DINOSAUR FACT DIG

TYRANNOSAURUS REX AND ITS RELATIVES
THE NEED-TO-KNOW FACTS

BY
MEGAN COOLEY PETERSON

Consultant: Mathew J. Wedel, PhD
Associate Professor
Western University of Health Services

raintree
a Capstone company — publishers for children

Raintree is an imprint of Capstone Global Library Limited, a company incorporated in England and Wales having its registered office at 264 Banbury Road, Oxford, OX2 7DY – Registered company number: 6695582

www.raintree.co.uk
myorders@raintree.co.uk

Edited by Michelle Hasselius
Designed by Kazuko Collins
Picture research by Wanda Winch
Production by Gene Bentdahl

ISBN 978 1 474 71941 4
20 19 18 17 16
10 9 8 7 6 5 4 3 2 1

British Library Cataloguing in Publication Data
A full catalogue record for this book is available from the British Library.

ACKNOWLEDGEMENTS
All images by Jon Hughes except: MapArt (maps), Shuttershock: Elena Elisseeva, green gingko leaf, Jiang Hongyan, yellow gingko leaf, Taigi, paper background

Every effort has been made to contact copyright holders of material reproduced in this book. Any omissions will be rectified in subsequent printings if notice is given to the publisher.

All the internet addresses (URLs) given in this book were valid at the time of going to press. However, due to the dynamic nature of the internet, some addresses may have changed, or sites may have changed or ceased to exist since publication. While the author and publisher regret any inconvenience this may cause readers, no responsibility for any such changes can be accepted by either the author or the publisher.

Printed in China.

CONTENTS

Roar! Tyrannosaurus rex was one of the fiercest dinosaurs that ever lived. This deadly hunter had sharp teeth and strong jaws. But did you know that a birdlike dinosaur with no teeth was related to T. rex?

Tyrannosaurus rex and its relatives lived between 160 and 65 million years ago. This group includes the toothless Gallimimus and the powerful Daspletosaurus. Some T. rex relatives hunted dinosaurs. Others ate insects and fruit. Each was amazing in its own way.

ALBERTOSAURUS

PRONOUNCED: al-BURR-toe-SAWR-us

NAME MEANING: Alberta reptile; fossils were discovered in Alberta, Canada

TIME PERIOD LIVED: Late Cretaceous Period, about 70 million years ago

LENGTH: 8.6 metres (28.2 feet)

WEIGHT: 2.5 metric tons (2.8 tons)

TYPE OF EATER: carnivore

PHYSICAL FEATURES: sharp teeth, two fingers on each small arm

Geologist Joseph Burr Tyrrell discovered the first **ALBERTOSAURUS** fossil in 1884. It was Canada's first known meat-eating dinosaur.

ALBERTOSAURUS probably hunted in packs to attack large herbivores. Young Albertosaurus may have chased prey towards stronger adults.

Albertosaurus lived in what are now Montana, USA and Alberta, Canada.

ALBERTOSAURUS had 60 curved, serrated teeth. It mainly hunted herbivores, but it was also a scavenger.

where this dinosaur lived

N
W E
S

5

ALIORAMUS

PRONOUNCED: AL-ee-OH-rah-MUS

NAME MEANING: other branch

TIME PERIOD LIVED: Late Cretaceous Period, about 70 million years ago

LENGTH: 5.8 metres (19 feet)

WEIGHT: 680 kilograms (1,500 pounds)

TYPE OF EATER: carnivore

PHYSICAL FEATURES: long jaws, bumpy horns on nose, ran on two legs

ALIORAMUS was one of the biggest hunters of its time. But it was only about half the size of Tyrannosaurus rex.

Alioramus lived in the forests of what is now Mongolia.

N
W   E
S

where this dinosaur lived

ALIORAMUS had eyes that faced forward, like today's owls and other birds of prey.

ALIORAMUS had more than 75 teeth, the most of any tyrannosaur.

ALVAREZSAURUS

PRONOUNCED: AL-vah-rez-SAWR-us

NAME MEANING: Alvarez's reptile, in honour of historian Don Gregorio Alvarez

TIME PERIOD LIVED: Late Cretaceous Period, about 85 million years ago

LENGTH: 1 metre (3.3 feet)

WEIGHT: 3 kilograms (6.5 pounds)

TYPE OF EATER: carnivore

PHYSICAL FEATURES: long legs and tail, one strong claw on each hand

Similar to today's anteaters, **ALVAREZSAURUS** dug into ant nests with its strong claws. It may have also had a long tongue that it used to pull ants and termites from their nests.

Alvarezsaurus lived in what is now Argentina.

N
W — E
S

where this dinosaur lived

ALVAREZSAURUS was about the size of a turkey.

ALVAREZSAURUS belonged to a group of dinosaurs called Alvarezsaurs. Dinosaurs in this group had a single claw on each strong arm.

COELURUS

PRONOUNCED: SEE-lur-rus

NAME MEANING: hollow tail

TIME PERIOD LIVED: Late Jurassic Period, about 155 million years ago

LENGTH: 2.5 metres (8 feet)

WEIGHT: 15 kilograms (33 pounds)

TYPE OF EATER: carnivore

PHYSICAL FEATURES: long fingers and a very long tail

COELURUS could run away from large predators like Allosaurus.

COELURUS belonged to a group of dinosaurs called coelurosaurs. Dinosaurs in this group had larger brains than other dinosaurs their size.

Coelurus lived in what is now the USA, in Wyoming and Utah.

where this dinosaur lived

N
W
E
S

COELURUS hunted small animals and dinosaurs.

COMPSOGNATHUS

PRONOUNCED: COMP-sog-NAY-thus

NAME MEANING: delicate jaw

TIME PERIOD LIVED: Late Jurassic Period, about 150 million years ago

LENGTH: 1.2 metres (4 feet)

WEIGHT: 2.5 kilograms (5.5 pounds)

TYPE OF EATER: carnivore

PHYSICAL FEATURES: long legs and tail, lightweight body, short teeth

A **COMPSOGNATHUS** fossil was found with the skeleton of the fast-running lizard Bavarisaurus in its stomach.

COMPSOGNATHUS was about the size of a chicken.

COMPSOGNATHUS hunted small lizards and bugs.

Compsognathus lived in forests and on beaches in France and Germany.

N
W E
S

where this dinosaur lived

DASPLETOSAURUS

PRONOUNCED: das-PLEET-o-SAWR-us

NAME MEANING: frightful reptile

TIME PERIOD LIVED: Late Cretaceous Period, about 80 million years ago

LENGTH: 9 metres (30 feet)

WEIGHT: 2.5 metric tons (2.8 tons)

TYPE OF EATER: carnivore

PHYSICAL FEATURES: big, sharp teeth and a strong body

Daspletosaurus lived in what is now the USA, in Montana and New Mexico, and Alberta, Canada.

N
W **E**
S

where this dinosaur lived

DASPLETOSAURUS is more closely related to Tyrannosaurus rex than any other dinosaur.

Many **DASPLETOSAURUS** fossils were found with healed injuries. The injuries show the dinosaurs bit each other's noses.

Similar to today's lions, **DASPLETOSAURUS** lived and hunted in family packs. The packs killed large herbivores, such as Triceratops.

EOTYRANNUS

PRONOUNCED: EE-o-tye-RAN-us

NAME MEANING: dawn tyrant

TIME PERIOD LIVED: Early Cretaceous Period, about 130 million years ago

LENGTH: 4.5 metres (14.8 feet)

WEIGHT: 200 kilograms (441 pounds)

TYPE OF EATER: carnivore

PHYSICAL FEATURES: long legs and arms, had feathers but couldn't fly

EOTYRANNUS was one of the smallest meat-eating dinosaurs in Europe.

EOTYRANNUS hunted small dinosaurs and animals. It made quick, deep bites into its prey.

Close relatives of **EOTYRANNUS** were discovered in China. These dinosaurs had feathers.

Eotyrannus lived in what is now England.

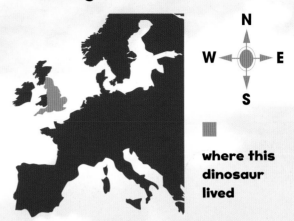

N
W E
S

where this dinosaur lived

EOTYRANNUS was named in 2001.

EOTYRANNUS could run fast. It used its speed to run away from bigger predators, such as Baryonx and Neovenator.

GALLIMIMUS

PRONOUNCED: GAL-i-MY-mus

NAME MEANING: chicken mimic

TIME PERIOD LIVED: Late Cretaceous Period, about 70 million years ago

LENGTH: 6 metres (20 feet)

WEIGHT: 450 kilograms (1,000 pounds)

TYPE OF EATER: omnivore

PHYSICAL FEATURES: long legs, beaklike snout with no teeth

GALLIMIMUS was hunted by predators such as Tarbosaurus bataar.

Similar to ostriches today, **GALLIMIMUS** could run very fast.

Gallimimus lived in the plains and forests of what is now Mongolia.

N
W E
S

where this dinosaur lived

GALLIMIMUS had comblike edges on its snout. The dinosaur may have used its snout to filter out food from rivers and lakes. It ate small animals, fruit and leaves.

GALLIMIMUS had three clawed fingers on each hand. Feathers covered the dinosaur's body.

GUANLONG

PRONOUNCED: gwahn-LONG

NAME MEANING: crowned dragon

TIME PERIOD LIVED: Late Jurassic Period, about 160 million years ago

LENGTH: 3 metres (9.8 feet)

WEIGHT: 113 kilograms (250 pounds)

TYPE OF EATER: carnivore

PHYSICAL FEATURES: colourful crest on its head, strong hands with a sharp claw on each finger

GUANLONG was a small dinosaur. It was about the size of a dog.

GUANLONG has the most complete skeleton of any early tyrannosauroid so far.

GUANLONG used its colourful crest to attract other dinosaurs.

Guanlong lived in what is now China.

N
W E
S

where this dinosaur lived

LABOCANIA

PRONOUNCED: LAB-o-KAN-ee-ah

NAME MEANING: La Bocana Roja lizard, because fossils were discovered at the La Bocana Roja Formation

TIME PERIOD LIVED: Late Cretaceous Period, about 75 million years ago

LENGTH: 7 metres (23 feet)

WEIGHT: 1.5 metric tons (1.7 tons)

TYPE OF EATER: carnivore

PHYSICAL FEATURES: thick snout and jaw, walked on two legs

Labocania lived in the forests of what is now Mexico.

N
W E
S

where this dinosaur lived

Only a few **LABOCANIA** fossils have been discovered, including a partial skull.

LABOCANIA had huge jaws and sharp teeth. One bite was often deadly.

LABOCANIA was the first theropod discovered in Mexico. Theropods were meat-eating dinosaurs that included tyrannosaurs, raptors and birds.

ORNITHOMIMUS

PRONOUNCED: OR-ni-thoh-MY-mus

NAME MEANING: bird mimic

TIME PERIOD LIVED: Late Cretaceous Period, about 65 million years ago

LENGTH: 3.5 metres (11.5 feet)

WEIGHT: 160 kilograms (350 pounds)

TYPE OF EATER: omnivore

PHYSICAL FEATURES: tiny head, long legs and neck, beak with no teeth

The dinosaur's body was covered with feathers. It looked like today's ostrich.

ORNITHOMIMUS had a beak covered with keratin. It ate fruit and insects.

Ornithomimus lived in what are now Colorado, Wyoming, South Dakota and Utah in the USA. This dinosaur also lived in Alberta and Saskatchewan, Canada.

In 1892 O.C. Marsh thought he had discovered a giant new species of **ORNITHOMIMUS**. He actually found the hip and leg bones of a Tyrannosaurus rex. These two dinosaurs had similar back leg bones.

where this dinosaur lived

N
W   E
S

TIMIMUS

PRONOUNCED: tee-MYE-mus

NAME MEANING: Tim's mimic, named after the son of the scientist who discovered it

TIME PERIOD LIVED: Early Cretaceous Period, about 100 million years ago

LENGTH: 3 metres (9.8 feet)

WEIGHT: 54 kilograms (120 pounds)

TYPE OF EATER: carnivore

PHYSICAL FEATURES: strong back legs, sharp claws

TIMIMUS fossils were discovered in Dinosaur Cove in southern Australia.

Scientists are not sure how to classify **TIMIMUS**. Some think it belonged to a group of dinosaurs called coelurosaurs. Dinosaurs in this group were hunters with narrow hands and large brains. Others think the dinosaur was an ornithomimosaur. These dinosaurs had small beaks and did not hunt.

TIMIMUS may have hibernated during the winter. Australia was closer to the South Pole during the Cretaceous Period.

Timimus lived in what is now Australia.

where this dinosaur lived

N
W E
S

TYRANNOSAURUS REX

PRONOUNCED: tie-RAN-ah-SAWR-us REX

NAME MEANING: king tyrant reptile

TIME PERIOD LIVED: Late Cretaceous Period, about 70 million years ago

LENGTH: 12 metres (40 feet)

WEIGHT: 8.2 metric tons (9 tons)

TYPE OF EATER: carnivore

PHYSICAL FEATURES: big head with sharp teeth, tiny arms, sharp claws and a long tail

TYRANNOSAURUS REX had excellent vision.

TYRANNOSAURUS REX was a predator that spent most of its time hunting. This dinosaur was also a scavenger.

TYRANNOSAURUS REX was the largest dinosaur in this group.

Tyrannosaurus rex lived in western North America.

N
W E
S

where this dinosaur lived

GLOSSARY

BEAK hard, pointed part of an animal's mouth

CARNIVORE animal that eats only meat

CREST flat plate of bone

CRETACEOUS PERIOD third period of the Mesozoic Era; the Cretaceous Period was from 145 to 65 million years ago

FOSSIL remains of an animal or plant from millions of years ago that have turned to rock

HERBIVORE animal that eats only plants

HIBERNATE spend winter in a deep sleep; animals hibernate to survive low temperatures and lack of food

JURASSIC PERIOD second period of the Mesozoic Era; the Jurassic Period was from 200 to 145 million years ago

KERATIN hard substance that makes up a person's fingernails and toenails

OMNIVORE animal that eats both plants and animals

PACK small group of animals that hunts together

PREDATOR animal that hunts another animal for food

PREY animal hunted by another animal for food

PRONOUNCE say a word in a certain way

SCAVENGER animal that eats animals that are already dead

SERRATED saw-toothed

SNOUT long front part of an animal's head; the snout includes the nose, mouth and jaws

COMPREHENSION QUESTIONS

1. How did Eotyrannus stay safe around large predators such as Baryonx and Neovenator?

2. Scientists are not sure how to classify Timimus. What two dinosaur groups could this dinosaur belong to?

3. Only a few Labocania fossils have been discovered. What is a fossil?

READ MORE

Dinosaurs (First Facts), Charlie Gardner (DK Publishing, 2012)

Tyrannosaurus Rex (All About Dinosaurs), Daniel Nunn (Raintree, 2015)

Tyrannosaurus Rex and other Giant Carnivores (Dinosaurs!), David West (Franklin Watts, 2013)

WEBSITES

www.nhm.ac.uk/discover/dino-directory/index.html

At this Natural History Museum website you can learn more about dinosaurs through sorting them by name, country and even body shape!

www.show.me.uk/section/dinosaurs

This website has loads of fun things to do and see, including a dinosaur mask you can download and print, videos, games, and Top Ten lists.

INDEX